Macaroni On A Hotdog

By
Sandra Oian Thomas

DEDICATION

I would like to dedicate this play to my parents Janet Marie (Ferden) Oian and Stanley Robert Oian. They paid for my college education, and have both said they are proud of me. :)

CONTENTS

ACKNOWLEDGMENTS

This play came about because I purchased a beautiful brides dress at a local thrift shop. I've been married for many years, with no plans to get re-married. Our house is packed to the gills with other such 'treasures' and I knew I had to justify the dress's existence. So I wrote the first monologue of this play, to bring to The Actors Workout , utilizing the brides dress as my costume... A huge thank you to Raye Birk and his Actors Workout at the Guthrie Theater where I developed this show. Raye Birk and my colleagues in class were invaluable as a sounding board and the Actor's Workout is a safe place to explore new work.

Mid-July, the 2014 Minnesota Fringe office called to tell me that there was a performance spot open. (I had been on a 'wait list', and was not expecting to be a part of the Fringe in 2014).
I would not have been able to put together this show in two weeks if some wonderful theatre artists/friends hadn't pitched in.

Shelli Place, Barbara Shelton, Elena Gianetti, MaryJo Pehl,
Mark Copenhaver, Frances Mae Copenhaver, Laurie Beth Fitz and local radio station AM950, Tom Michlitsch, Lorna Landvik, Melinda Kordich, Tom Winner, Phyllis Wright, Neal Beckman, Colleen Barrett, Tony Cammarata, Tyler Driskill, Billy Johnston, Andy Peterson, Mabel Thomas, and Walter Young. Lastly I would like to thank my husband Glenn Thomas for his affection, encouragement, sperm, and financial and technical support.

Cover photo by Barbara Shelton

PLAY HISTORY

The first production of Macaroni On A Hotdog occurred on July 31st, 2014 at the Playwright's Center Theater in Minneapolis Minnesota.

Cast: Sandra Thomas
Director: Shelli Place
Producer: Sandra Thomas
Assistant Producer: Elena Gianetti
Sound Design: Mark Copenhaver

Characters
(In Order of Appearance)
Lisa

Raphney

Wedding Singer (The Band)

Victoria Johnson

Douglas Johnson

Patricia (Patty) Larson

The set: Written as a one-woman 'fringe' show. A small lightweight table is used for Raphney's guest book, and then moved to be the table Douglas will stand beside to make his toast. A chair is used for Patty, the final bride.

Props/Costumes: A brief description of each character precedes their first line. Dialogue for Raphney can be shaped to reflect whatever type of hand knit vest you can find. A walker for Raphney. An asthma inhaler and boom box with microphone (which does not have to be functional) for the Wedding Singer. A paper napkin for Douglas to have his speech notes written on, and a disposable wine glass and knife. Patty will need a partially filled Boone's Farm wine bottle. For the music (for the three original songs the Wedding Singer performs) feel free to make up your own tunes.

Playwrights Notes: The first production of Macaroni on a Hotdog, was for the Minneapolis Fringe Festival in 2014. It was in the top ten shows (out of 169).
The closer you can get to making each character a real person (and not a caricature) the funnier the play will be.

About the playwright: Sandra Thomas has written historical plays, 'The Crimson Prairie', 'Gideon Pond and His Red Nation', 'Highland Prairie Cemetery Walk 1864-2004', and 'Chains of Slavery'. Also a 10 minute play about bullying 'Son of Scrap Iron', and has written and directed several short films.

MACARONI ON A HOTDOG

ACT I

Scene 1

Lights Up: *A woman in a beautiful brides dress enters. Although she has a pretty dress on, no particular care has been taken with her hair or makeup. She carries a binder with "Department of Corrections" logo on cover.*

LISA

Thank you for having me here today. My speaking with you will count towards an additional 2 hours of my court ordered 500 hours of community service. . . .I have currently served 212 hours. My name is Lisa, and 4 years ago I had a wedding.

My wedding day was July 1st, 2010. The outdoor ceremony took place at 2 P.M., in a metro park. I had failed to plan. . .anticipate. . . .for extreme heat. . . . since the wedding guests were seated in direct sunlight that time of day. I'm now **required** to read you ... the following. (*Opens binder*) My willful neglect of the safety and comfort of others is what brings me here today. Because of my actions . . . I put lives at risk. Especially the elderly.

A momentary glance at typical weather patterns for that day and time, would have shown that temperatures are often in the high 90's. Even a smart phone or iPad (I have both) could have researched possible weather conditions.

The court ruled that I was obviously concerned with my own comfort and pleasure, since I had hired a luxury air-conditioned bus, at a cost of several thousand dollars, to transport myself and 6 bridesmaids and groomsmen (just the wedding party). . . on a 3 hour scenic tour. While all the invited guests were abandoned in the extreme heat and humidity. . . left to their own devices - until the reception and dance, later that night.

As a result of this inattention several guests were treated at the Urgent Care Clinic for dehydration and heat exhaustion, or sunstroke.

The consequences of this thoughtless behavior, brought about a class action suit filed by most of the guests at my wedding. The subsequent very public trial and judgment led to these cautionary talks I am now giving to young people. . . such as yourselves.

It also led to Minnesota Statute 107.1, also known as Lisa's Law, which sets firm guidelines that weddings are now required to adhere to.

Slide shows of the bride at groom at the reception may not exceed 20 minutes. Particularly if they contain childhood or baby pictures. Every minute in excess of the 20 minute time limit, entitles wedding guests to an unlimited (or bottomless) glass of alcohol. Or in the case of a non-drinker, the cash equivalent.

If a microphone is deployed and speeches are given, any inebriated relative of the bridal couple, who's been drinking since noon, will be allowed a maximum of 5 minutes to tell her emotion filled story of how her sister the bride, drove 140 miles to pick her up in Iowa that one time she was in that car accident.

If personal stories with a microphone exceed 20 minutes, wedding guests are under no obligation to remain, and takeout containers with their meal shall be supplied. Any speechifying past 30 minutes, the guests are allowed to grab any present of their choosing, on their way out the door.

Seating arrangements specify that the bride may not seat guests according to who she likes best at that particular moment. For example: my Uncle Doug and his wife....Cindi (who happen to both be attorneys, may not be seated in the most remote corner of the room, if all the other relatives are seated in close proximity to the bridal couple. Reasonable care must be taken, or punitive liability exists.

Wearing my dress for todays appearance, costs $158.76. Amortized over the length of my community service. It was a very expensive dress, and a big part of the reason for my eventual bankruptcy.

If you are currently engaged, and find yourself using phrases like "It's the most important day of my life." or "It's my one chance to be a princess." You may be in need of an intervention and I urge you to get the help you need, before it's too late.

I'd like to thank Mrs.Hanson and her entire 5th grade class for having me here today. Many of you will get married yourselves someday - so remember this cautionary tale and avoid the misery my ex-husband and I now find ourselves in.

Thank you

I can answer a few questions and I'll call on you by the nametags on the front of your desks.

Yes . . . Caden M. First off, the term jailbird is highly offensive. I'd prefer felon. My time served was very educational. . . I read several books and wrote this speech, so it was time well spent.

Caden R. No, I am not allowed to vote, but I didn't vote before I got convicted.

Final question.

Amber W. No, I did not keep the ring. It went straight to the thrift store when I broke out in a rash because of the high nickel content. The stone wasn't even a diamond. . . It was cheaper than cubic zirconium. . . .I'd urge all prospective brides to PICK OUT THE RING IN PERSON!!! To avoid finding out later that's its worth less than 30 bucks.

Lights out

CHARACTER exits

Audio plays while Raphney changes into costume for the wedding singer.

Audio: - *The TwoTonys - July 2010*

Tony: Good morning! It's the 'two Tony's' on K-F-A-M in the morning and it's gonna be a hot one today! Tony, what's the temp?

Toni: 99 degrees and climbing Tony.

Tony: whooo doggies, time to crack that egg on the sidewalk.

Toni: according to the weather service, July of 2010 is turning into the hottest one on record!

Tony: That's right Toni, it's the first of July and we're breaking records left and right. If you don't have to be out in this heat, stay home!

Toni: Absolutely! Open a cold one and sit in front of your fan.

Tony: I know just which fan I want to sit in front of too. Her name is Sherice. (they crack up)

Toni: Don't go there Tony, don't go there.

Tony: Hey now, we've got the 4th of July coming up in a couple of days, what kind of weather are we expecting? More of the same?

Toni: Hot and humid all week, according to our own Kevin Dunbar, KFAMs meteorologist to the stars....

Tony: Kevin knows about ALL things weather Tony, he went to college and everything! All right, we've got some great music coming up at the top of the hour, but first let's hear from Rob with quick look at metro traffic.

Scene 2

Lights Up: *Raphney enters. An octogenarian pushing a walker. She has completely grey hair, and glasses. She wears a short-sleeved white turtleneck and a hand knit purple and white striped vest, the kind that might have been popular in the 1970's. Lavender/purple pants that match the vest and comfortable shoes. Minnesota accent a plus.*

RAPHNEY

O.K. girls, we got a full blown emergency upstairs. The wedding food is ruined, and the bride and groom are gone! All the guests from Lisa and Eric's outdoor wedding in the park across the street are crowding into the church banquet hall upstairs. There's no sign of the bride and groom, Evelyn said they're on a bus or something? It seems kinda strange they're not at their own reception. We can't even cut the cake. . .

The wedding guests are expecting food, but that ice sculpture. . . .I told 'em, on a hot day like this, them ice sculptures start to melt the minute you take 'em out of the freezer. It was like puttin' lemon bars under Niagara Falls. Ooooo it's hot, I'm close to takin off my summer vest entirely. The air conditioner is just not working properly, and you can't even open the stained glass up there to catch a breeze. I'll tell ya. Now this is our chance to shine ladies! When the Mary Circle got all the credit for the quilting last winter, that was one thing, and the Ruth Circle did such a nice job cleaning up the parsonage. They really did. Now I know they have youth on their side - most of em aren't even retired.

But the Dorcas Circle has heart. Well yeah, heart problems, and arthritis, ileitis, gall stones, diver tick u lie tus, and some of our girls aren't even fully ambulatory, but I think we can really save the day here, if we just focus and PULL TOGETHER.

Oh, say, I sure like those loafers Shirley. They look so comfortable. Are they Hush Puppies? I had a pair of Hush Puppies that I just wore out I loved em so much.

They were gray, but a lighter gray, so I wore em all year. My daughter gave em to me.

No. . . the younger one, she's so thoughtful - yeah - she's married to the grade school principal, they have the 2 boys, it's my older daughter that has just the one girl.

I think it's harder to have just the one - they got no one to play with, and to tell you the truth they get kinda spoilt - no competition. Oh Gee, where was I? Oh, ya, the food. . . . upstairs, they're using the punch bowl ladle and putting MELTED jello in their glasses and drinking it! It's colorful, but it can't taste that good. Everything else is just shot. . . soggy and limp. . . . it's a table full of mush. It's up to us to feed that crowd before they start to faint or something. We'll show that Mary Circle how it's done! Can someone yell in Evelyn's good ear that we're gonna need to cook now? O.K. Mavis and Norma can you throw open those cupboards so we can see what we've got? Many many many boxes of Creamette elbow macaroni. They must have got that at the Cub, you know it goes down to $1.29 a lot there lately, and sometimes they'll even put it on the buy one get one FREE. I stock up! (sigh)
O.K. We got noodles. What else? Marion can you look in the fridge? Shirley can you hand Marion her walker?
Weeenies!!! Oh, nice. They must all be for the Luther League 4th of July. Well, I know its not Luther League anymore. What do they. . . .Oh, HIGH League. Why is that? Is that just another attempt to ease Martin Luther out of his own church? The Luthern church? It's LUTHER LEAGUE, that's what they called it when my kids went and that's what I call it. O.K. Here's what we'll do. We cook them noodles and decorate 'em with the weenies! Just like the Cake Boss. Can somebody help Mavis with that elbow macaroni? I forgot about your frozen shoulder ...she can't get it up past here (indicates how far Mavis can raise her arm). Oh that's great, Norma found some cherry tomatoes. So, noodles first, then a weenie and then a couple of cherry tomatoes at the base of the weenie. (The hand gestures indicate an erect vertical hotdog, with tomato testicles) It's gonna look every bit as fancy as any of your high tone restaurants. Just like the Perkins.

Lights Out

CHARACTER exits

Audio: - Impound Lot

We hear the sound of someone pressing touchtone phone buttons, and then the sound of a phone ringing.

Louie: Municipal Impound lot.
Cynthia : Please tell me you have my car. I'm at my husbands' nieces wedding, and I think I got food poisoning from the food. I just want to go home, but my car isn't where I left it! I parked on the street in front of the church, the invitation said I could park there.
Louie:: What's the color....make, model.... license of the vehicle?
Cynthia : it's a green Lexus. License number THX-1138
Louie: Hang on. . . .Gary, green Lexus THX-1138? (Pause) Yeah. It's here. You'll need to bring a valid drivers license, current car title or rental agreement, proof of insurance, and 285 dollars in cash if the vehicle is picked up before 6 PM today. And we can't take a credit card, cuz the systems down.
Cynthia: That's 10 minutes from now!!!
Louie: (beat) My clock says 8.
Cynthia: How am I supposed to get there? You have my car!
Louie: Find a friend. . . call a cab.
Cynthia : I have no money. I'm carrying a tiny purse, the kind you can just fit a lipstick and license in. Oh good lord... the best man just threw up on my shoe.
Louie: Like I said lady....find a friend.
Cynthia : I have no friends here ...just family.

Scene 3

Lights up: *Enter, the Wedding Singer. She is an aspiring entertainer, with
              ambition the size of Dolly and talent the size of your cousin … the one
              that entertains family members by playing her clarinet at Thanksgiving.
              She is dressed in sparkly attire. The more sparkles, the better, and
              high-heeled boots are a plus. Also. . . a southern accent. She uses the
              microphone, even though it doesn't amplify sound.*

WEDDING SINGER

Can I have your attention please? Usually someone would introduce me,
but there's a number of people involved in this wedding who've taken ill, so
I'll just introduce myself. I am the band. Here's to Erik and Lisa, the bride
and groom. I have known Erik a long time, and I lofff… I really like him,
and I don't know Lisa well enough to not like her yet. So, here's to Erik
…and Lisa! Normally the best man would give the wedding toast, but as
y'all know he was taken to the hospital. . . when he. . . well some people
seem to think he fainted, but he mighta passed out. I know all the
groomsmen & let me tell you, they KNOW how to party. Most of em,
including the groom, are regulars at my club. Well it's not MY club, my
uncle owns it really. Let me tell you - if you want a career in show business,
it helps to have your uncle own a club. He doesn't pay me (yet) but that's
what I'm workin' towards. Erik IS payin me, I am gettin paid for today,
this is my first official gig, although I have won SEVERAL karaoke
contests, and as you know SEVERAL means more than two.
Now this first song is real special - cuz it's the one that Lisa starts out by
dancing with her daddy and then Erik cuts in & everybody gets real choked
up. Erik you are ON DECK, quit your grab assin' with the bridesmaids.
We are havin' some problems with the power - so I'll be singin' arcapella -
which as you know - means without a boombox.

(Sings)

*Home is where the fart is
I eat beans all the time
My eyes have lost their sparkle
My hair has lost it's shine*

Please come back
And share my love
I promise I'll be clean
I'll bathe and sweep and keep our nest
Why did you treat me mean?

Thank you

Normally at my club, Uncle John's club, (Rumbles on route 23) I sing between the dancers, Sunday through Tuesday, at noon, and I am a legitimate singer, I do not take my clothes off. Unless someone keeps tellin' me they love me. Right Erik?
Love is what brings us here today - no one was more surprised than me, to find out Erik was gettin married - - - - - He did NOT act engaged at Rumble's. I suppose him hirin' me to sing at his weddin was sort of a consolation prize.
As you know - consolation means your friends console you when you find out your boyfriends engaged.
I'd like to dedicate this next song to the groom.

(Sings)

Like a burnt and crusty marshmallow you take off of your stick
Our love is like a s'more gone bad, and you are such a dick
You shouldn't oughta treat me bad, and look the other way,
I'd let you have the last s'more if you would only stay

S'more love
S'more love
I just want
S'more love

Thank you

For the final song in my rep a twhar (which is French) and as you know, means the 3 songs I can do, I'll be takin a break after this next song - my asthma is acting up -
I am SEVERELY allergic to dogs & there is a dog eating off that buffet table
(I don't thing that's sanitary)

(Sings)

When you left
I wasn't certain
(Wheeze)

Couldn't think
Cuz I was hurtin'

(Wheeze, and has to use the inhaler)
I can't breathe
I'm sorry
(breath)
By the way Eric. . . . I'm late

Lights out

CHARACTER exits

Audio: - 911 Call

Phone dialing audio, then the phone ringing audio

911:   911 what is your emergency?

Carol: There's so many I don't know where to start. 5 or 6 people have fainted, the bathrooms quit working, because so many people are vomiting or having diarrhea. It looks like a war zone!
911: Ma'am I'm dispatching two ambulances, can you verify your location for me?
Carol: We're at Highland Avenue Lutheran Church, it's right across the street from the park. But you can only get there on 26th street cuz there's road construction all down Highland. It's right by where the old Dairy Queen used to be before they built that strip mall on Fremont. Everyone's sick, you might need to send the police too, there's a fist fight going on in the parking lot. The brides father Dewey... is drunk again....and he got in a car.. I don't know whose, I don't even think he's allowed to have a drivers license.... and he tried backing out of the parking lot and he smashed into a ton of cars and just took off. The parking lot looks like a demolition derby.
911: A squad car is on it's way. Is it possible for you to stand in front of the building to help flag down the ambulance?
Carol: I think so... I'll try... I need to find a trash can or a bowl though, I feel nauseous . . . and dizzy...I think I'm gonna be sick....(Phone drops)

911: Ma'am? Hello!??

Scene 4

Lights up: *Enter Victoria. Blonde dreadlocks, Lululemon yoga capri's,*
                  Birkenstock sandals (the iconic ones) and a Prana yoga shirt.
                  Approximating an urban hipster, Victoria relies heavily on the trust
                  fund her wealthy parents have established for her. She is able to fund
                  her pets, her causes, her lifestyle, without having to work. Her pain is
                  real at losing her pet.

VICTORIA

Hello Everyone, I'm Victoria Johnson. Welcome to my home. I'd like to
thank all of you for coming here today. I'm surprised so many of you were
recovered enough to drive to my house for today's celebration of life. It's
been a tough couple of days since my cousin Lisa's wedding. I actually
don't believe in miracles. Because I don't believe there's a 'divine force'
that oversees this world, but if I get through this celebration of life without
crying, it will be the closest thing to an atheist's miracle there is.
 I was told. . . she didn't suffer. The end came quickly, and decisively for
one so young, and so healthy.
When I put the word out - on social media. . . Facebook. . . Twitter. . .
Instagram, Tumbler.. . about today's celebration of life. . . I knew my
friends would show up. I even see friends of friends. . and friends I've
unfriended..... (sorry). No matter how often my family disappoints me,
my friends have always been there for me.
I'd like to thank so many of you who've sent these elaborate floral tributes.
The orchids, the roses. . . So beautiful....
The food is fabulous, and it's all you can eat, so please have as much as
you'd like. Who doesn't like an Indian Buffet with all the chutneys and two
kinds of naan. On my deck there are desserts from Patrick's Bakery, red
velvet cupcakes, Sara Cake, Tiaramisu. Vegan options abound for all of my
friends who appreciate 'cruelty free' food.
It's all so good. No expense was spared to honor a life that's touched us all.
For many of us here. . . with Sierra's passing. . . our lives will never be the
same.
When my parents had their 30th wedding anniversary celebration, they took
a cruise. They brought along the whole family, spouses included. Sierra
wasn't invited. . . and that hurt. But having you show up here today
mother, with your little 2 dollar clump of flowers from Trader Joe's, goes a
long way toward healing that memory, and building a bridge. My father
Douglas can't be here, he is still recuperating from the food poisoning that
so many of us endured, ...

I don't want to dwell on past hurts, and recrimination. (I'll save that for your eulogy mother). That's what not today is about. . . that's not what honors a beautiful life - extinguished.

We've been entertained, and moved this afternoon, by some amazing poetry and dance.

I'd like to thank De'Sean Jehova for his tone poem. And the Double Amputee Dance Ensemble of Wayzata for their interpretive dance entitled 'Memory and Loss'. Sierra would have loved this so much. She loved people.

Conspicuously absent is any condolence from my cousin Lisa. My cousin Lisa, who hosted a lethal wedding. Presumably she and Erik are having fun on their honeymoon. In Belize.

Not even a text saying "sorry about your dog."

Sorry about that TOXIC chocolate fountain we had at our wedding. FOUNTAIN OF DEATH!

It would have hurt a LOT less if we'd even been made to feel welcome at that wedding. Sierra's...last...wedding.

After they saw my beautiful dog, we weren't even allowed to sit with the rest of the family. They sat us by the EXIT, because someone, somewhere had an ALLERGY.

They were so surprised Sierra was a dog, and not my partner. Guess what Lisa? I'm not gay! There are any number of friends I could have brought along as my 'date'. But none of them are as fun as my dog.

Everyone LOVES Sierra. . . . . loved Sierra.

I'd like to draw your attention to the sign up sheet located next to the Shiraz. I know there are many people here who were affected by my cousin Lisa's wedding. Food poisoning, heat stroke... towing fees for the people that were told ON THE INVITATION, that they could park on the street, right by the church. It's there, in black and white, and they are going to make this right. My parents Douglas and Cynthia Johnson are BOTH attorney's and they have agreed to manage a class action lawsuit on behalf of anyone hurt at Lisa's wedding. Please put the word out, and take some business cards with the "sue Erik & Lisa" hotline number.

Now before anyone leaves today, we are going to do something beautiful, to honor the memory of a dog that took joy and gave joy during every moment of her time here on earth. We are going to raise some money to landscape my yard. We are putting in trees and bushes for all of Sierras dog friends....

The landscaper's design (hold up blueprint) calls for maples along the front yard, interspersed with lilacs, and a formal boxwood meditation maze on my side yard with a complementary doggie poo bag dispenser. And a statue of Sierra... in bronze.... (getting choked up) her favorite metal.

Who will buy the first tree. . . . .for Sierra.

(excruciating pause)

Thank you mother.
We just have 10 trees and 134 bushes to go. We'll stay here until it's done.

                                                    CHARACTER exits

Audio: - *The Two Tonys - June 1988*

Clip of Huey Lewis' "Back In Time"

Tony: And that was a little bit of Huey Lewis and The News' "Back In Time".
Toni: Back in time, wow.
Tony: You know it's coming out of that "Back To The Future" soundtrack. That is HOT!
Toni: That IS hot! And I would like to say that he is quite good looking!
Tony: He is a handsome devil, I must say.
Toni: He is!
Tony: You know that was on the Billboard charts this week coming in at about number 27.
Toni: You know Tony, we have had the hottest rockin songs this year.
Tony: We really have in fact it kinda reminds me, oh by the way, I was just looking at my announcements for the day calendar.
Toni: Yeah?
Tony: June 6th forty four years ago, D-Day!
Toni Ohhh, D-Day...
Tony: The troops stormed Normandy.
Toni: That's right! What does the D stand for?
Tony: You know what? I don't know, but I think somebody out there in our listening audience probably does.
Toni: Yeah. Call in.
Tony: Give us a call, let us know. Anybody out there Playing Trivial Pursuit on this beautiful day?
Toni: Hey what's your favorite piece?
Tony: The pie.
Laughter
Toni: Yum, yum!
Toni: What's your favorite pie?
Tony: Uh, Key Lime.
Toni: Strawberry-Rhubarb!
Tony: Ooh, I love that except sometimes it can be a little Tart.
Toni: Gotta add more Sugar!
Fade in Billy Idol's "White Wedding"
Tony: (Talking over the music) You know what? What kind of a day is it?
Toni: It's a nice day.
Tony: For a White Wedding! Here's some Billy Idol!

Scene 5

Lights up: *Enter Rapheny 20 years earlier. Instead of completely gray, she is salt and pepper gray, same glasses, same pants and vest, but a different shirt and Hush Puppies on her feet. She uses no walker and has more energy and talks slightly faster.*

RAPHNEY

Would you like to sign the guest book? Well thank you, the vest is new. My cousin Janet knit it for me. It's her husband that's got the black toe.....you can't fool around with diabetes. And I do feel bad for him, but they told him 5 years ago he should quit smoking. Janet made me matching pot holders for this vest too, but I don't even want to use 'em they're so nice!. I put 'em way back in the drawer so nobody slobs hot dish on 'em. I'll save em for company. The corsage is from the bride and groom of course... and you are not gonna believe this, but these are fake flowers! They're fabric, but they look so real, and they'll just last forever. I'll be able to wear them to other weddings. I can probably just put em in my purse, (in a Baggie) and as long as they blend in with whatever wedding I'm attending. . .BINGO, I'll feel like the belle of the ball.
People don't wear corsages as much as they used to, but it's such a festive thing, doncha think?
I've got new shoes on today too. My daughter Karen in Ohio, she's got the two kids, her husband is the 5th grade teacher, but he's getting his masters degree to be a principal someday. Karen's got her teaching certificate too, but she's staying home with the boys while they're young, well she sent me these Hush Puppies, for my birthday, and they are SO comfortable. It feels like I'm wearing angora mittens on my feet. The color is so nice too, they go with anything. The only thing I won't wear them with is my swimsuit. . . and that's because I don't want water spots on em. Suede, you know. Isnt' it fun to get dressed up in new clothes? I feel just like Grace Kelly today with so many new things on. The pants I've had for awhile. They're a cotton/poly blend so I don't have to iron em. Unless I forget em in the dryer. I don't care how much they stress it's a no-iron fabric, if you leave em in the dryer overnight you'll see some wrinkles.
I was sure tickled to be asked to help with this wedding. I think it was a bit of a 'rush job' though. I've never gotten a wedding invitation on a post card before. Spose that saved em a bit on postage.
Oh, did you see the cake yet? That's sure different. I guess those are little professional wrestler figures on the top of it.

When Ernie and I got married (well you were there) we just had a small cake, real simple, remember? Those roses made out of frosting? We had those. . . white ones, but then he was shipping out for basic training the next day. So we kept things simple. Funny how styles change. I wouldn't have thought to put a celebrity on my cake. I bet Ernie would have liked to have Dorothy Lamour on our cake, he always liked her. Probably those sarongs. I always liked Spanky from the Our Gang comedies, but Spanky and Dorothy wouldn't really make a good couple. She could babysit him, but I don't think she'd wanna marry him.

Oh say you'd better let me go Gloria, there's getting to be quite a line behind you. . . There's Lorraine. Hi Lorraine!! and Ardis. Hi girls!! We can catch up during the reception Gloria, say... can you save me some of them pastel colored butter mints? Those are my favorites. . . see you later then. Well hello Arlene, don't you look nice today. Would you like to sign the guest book? Well thank you, yes the vest is new. My cousin Janet hand knit this for me. She's got the arthritis in her hands, but she still manages to keep busy. That's probably a good thing too, they say the motion is the lotion.

Lights out

CHARACTER exits

Audio: - *Wedding Ushers*

Usher 1: Did you see Slappy?

Usher 2: I saw what's left of him.

Usher 1: Poor guy....never saw this comin.

Usher 2: I think he missed a bullet on this deal.

Usher 1: You ever been an usher before?

Usher 2: No.

Usher 1: Just ask 'em brides side, or grooms side. Lookin' at
the alter Patty's side is on the left, and Dingers side is on the right.
Where's your flower?

Usher 2: Didn't get one.

Usher 1: Dingers aunt Raphney has em. She's the lady at the guest book,
Ask for your flower... But do not under ANY circumstances say anything
about her vest.

Usher 2: Huh?

Usher 1: Trust me. I'll take over til you get back... Hi...which side are you
on?

Mabel: What?

Usher 1: Are you on the brides side, or the grooms side?

Mabel: Why, what happened?

Usher 1: Do you want to sit on the bride's side, or the groom's side for the
ceremony.

Mabel: You guys, he wants to know what side we're on.

Ella: Why?

Elizabeth: What?

Mabel: We have to pick a side to sit on.

Ella; But we're friends of both of them. Is there a middle side?

Elizabeth: There's fewer people on Dinger's side.

Mabel: I remember when my mom got re-married, almost nobody was on
her side.

It was sad.

Ella: Yeah. . . . but if Patty sees us sitting on Dingers side, she's gonna be
pissed.

Elizabeth (to the usher): Brides side.

Mabel: Me too...I don't want my car keyed...again.

Scene 6

Lights up: *Enter Douglas. Dressed in khaki pants, suit coat and tie*
              with preppy loafers. Moustache is optional. He is full of
              himself.

DOUGLAS

Hello I'm Douglas Johnson, brother of Mrs. Patricia Larson (née Johnson)
today's bride. My parents have asked me to step in and deliver the best man's
toast, since the actual best man is . . . indisposed. Apparently 15 is the limit
of jello shots a grown man can do, before lunch.
My sister Patricia and I have never been particularly close, but now is not the
time to air family grievances. I'll save that for your eulogy Patricia. (laugh)
Oh, sorry. . . . . Patty. My sister has never liked her 'given' name, she prefers
Patty. Like the hamburger...or the cake.
I've made some notes.
When Patty first started dating Slappy, I was taken aback. I hadn't ever
imagined myself having a brother-in-law called Slappy. I needn't have
worried though, because although Slappy had his moment... it was ultimately
the charms of Dinger, Slappy's best friend, which won the day. Dinger's
charms were more than Patty could resist. So now at the ripe old age of 17,
Patty is pledging her troth to . . . Dinger aka Duane aka Dewey...according to
his mother, the family call him Dewey.
Having so many aliases may come in handy for the wedding couple, in the
decades to come. (chuckle). I have not been home to witness their brief and
tempestuous courtship, having just completed my first year at William
Mitchell School of Law. I plan to be a practicing attorney by spring of
1990...I envision plenty of pro-bono work in the future, on behalf of the
bridal couple... having already advised them regarding disputed rights over
some Ramones tapes the groom lent to a friend. (laugh)
My sister and I are five years and one hundred eighty degrees apart. (chuckle)
The siren song of academia has always called to me, whereas Patty has
perpetually preferred partying. A social life, over school. I wish her well, in
the life she's chosen. She's been running toward this life since her freshman
year, when she dated 'Wipeout'. The 26 year old high school dropout who'd
park his van across from the high school to sell dope to kids during lunch. I
know my parents were relieved when that relationship went south. Literally.
Wipeout is now at Stillwater Correctional Facility, serving 10 to 12 for being a
sexual predator.

My interest in the law predates Wipeout. Having been sparked in childhood when some friends of my sister began shoplifting candy and trading cards from the local Gas-n-Gulp.

After researching possible legal consequences at the municipal library, I continually counseled my sister on her rights and responsibilities until she came to her senses and gave up those acquaintances. Thus began my enduring friendship with Mrs. Jenkins, our local librarian, who in fact wrote a letter of reference that was included in my successful application to law school.

Don't worry Duane, I freely relinquish all future responsibility for my sister, to you, as you begin your new life together.

The bride, is employed part time at the 8th street Tasty Freeze. And the groom works second shift at the dog food plant. Patty's dated men with a job before, but… seven consecutive weeks! Imagine the pension.

Patty and Dinger have qualified for a mortgage and after their honeymoon, in Nisswa… they will be moving into their 'double-wide' parked at the Pine View Trailer Court near Frazee.

Please raise your plastic disposable glass, partly filled with domestic sparkling wine. . .

Patty and Dinger… your future's so bright, you'll have to wear shades.

Lights outs

CHARACTER exits

Audio: - *Decorating The Van*

A: Ok where's the shaving cream?

B: Couldn't find it, brought a magic marker though.

C: Like the kind that's permanent?

B: I dunno.. Probably.

C: Dingers gonna be pissed.

A: It's funnier this way.

C: Whatever.

B: What're you tying to the bumper?

A: I made it in shop.

B: What is it?

A: I dunno, but I got a C+ on it.

C: Why do you tie stuff on the getaway car when someone gets married anyway?

B: (chuckles) So they have stuff to throw at each other when they fight

A: Look what else I got! (chuckle) I'm tying on what's left of our ice fishing house after Dewey got it off the lake this year

C: Geez, what happened? Did it fall off the trailer?

A: Dewey didn't use a trailer, he just put a rope around it, tied it to his van... And took off!

(Laughter)

B: So how far gone is Patty?

C: Right before he passed out Slappy told me she's 4 months along.

A: Man.... it's a good thing Dinger sucks at math.

Lights up: *Enter Patty. A cheaper, less stylish and less fitted brides dress. Also, it can have puffy sleeves and a Dynasty look to it. She's been drinking and is carrying a partially filled bottle of Boone's Farm wine. Her hair is 'rocker 80's' hair (think Rod Stewart).*

PATTY

Patty: Oh my God you guuuuuuys, I'm married!

It sucks I had to get married in June. I wanted a bouncy jiggler wedding, which would have been August 8th, 1988. 8-8-88!

You tip them 8's on their sides and put dots in the middle, it's boobs!!! We are the bouncy jigglers....jigglers RULE !!!

You guys are my best friends. I'm so glad there's 7 of you, so I could do rainbow bridesmaids. ROY-G-BIV jigglers!!!!! Rainbow bridesmaids is the only thing I wanted for my wedding, that I got.

I love you guys!

Who wants some Boone's Farm? It's not Tickled Pink. Slappy got me Strawberry Hill. I can't wait til I'm legal and then I can buy all the Tickle Pink I want.

Can you believe the sound guy for the church plays the EXTENDED VERSION of White Wedding!   Gawd, it felt like we were standing up there forever!

So I'm standing up there with nothing to do, and geez, I see Hekkeral in the audience and I'm like how can my math teacher be at my wedding? And I'm like oh, yeah, my dad knows him from Mason's and Demolay, and then GEEZ I'm remembering the pop quiz yesterday and knowing I totally TANKED because I freaked out about not remembering what an integer even is and I'm thinking I'll ask him when he shakes my hand if he wants to just pass me in Math for a wedding present, but then he goes "Congratulations Mrs. Larson" and I'm like looking around for Dingers mom, cuz SHE'S Mrs. Larson.

Oh my God, that music went on forever! (laughter) Dinger and me started playing "thumb wars" up there. The pastor even saw. We were all just crackin' up.

Oh my god I'm married....

I wanted pizza and chips for the reception and my parents are all "We're paying for this event, and that's not an appropriate supper, blah blah blah". I'd rather be at the kegger Jason and them are throwin down by the river. My parents wouldn't even let me invite Jason because of that stupid restraining order . (sigh)

It feels like there's WAY more of my parents friends here than mine. This wedding sucks. They wouldn't even let me have a chocolate wedding cake!!!

At least we got Hulk Hogan and Miss Elizabeth on the top of the cake. That was my idea. Miss Elizabeth should be with Hulk Hogan. He's way more of a gentleman than Savage.

You guys.... Dinger did the most romantic thing oh my god he had his mom make Jell-O shots for us!,

He got em for us you guys! they look like little boobs!!!! They're jiggler shots!!!! (laughter)

It's the most romantic thing he's ever done.

 Dinger and me didn't make any money on this wedding. I'm pretty sure I'll get some cash for graduation, but sometimes relatives just give you pens, or some lame book.

Who can help me separate the wedding presents? We need to make a pile of the ones that have price tags and receipts, I'm pretty sure we can return those for cash. So we registered for this really nice boombox, JVC, but we didn't get it. I think we're gonna use the cash we do get for a CD player for Dingers van.

 Oh my God you guys, my brother Doug is such a tight wad!! Just because I barfed in his new Chevette. Get over it. Pregnant people barf. That's what they do. His creepy new girlfriend knitted me a potholder for my bridal shower. I'm OVERWHELMED with gratitude. Not! Am I showing yet you guys? (turn sideways) I'm like 4 months along . . . So my brother Doug goes "My wedding gift to you Patricia is to not sue you for damages to my car." He's in his 1st year at Law School and he thinks he's Perry Mason or something. GEEZ! What an a-hole! He's pre-engaged to his snotty new girlfriend Cynthia... God help you if you call her Cindi...You know why her parents named her Cynthia? They didn't know how to spell blecchh!

I feel so fat!

I can't wait until I can wear my Calvin's again. So my mom keeps staring at my stomach and going (SIGH).   (Rolls her eyes) Yes, I get it, just put a scarlet thing on my face why don't you?

So I know THREE things you guys:

One. I'm having a girl (future jiggler!)

Two. I'm naming her Lisa (in honor of my favorite Lisa … Simpson)

and THREE, when she grows up, she is going to have the BEST WEDDING EVER! (soft giggle) Room spins…cool.

Lights out

End of play

www.ingramcontent.com/pod-product-compliance
Lightning Source LLC
Chambersburg PA
CBHW051002030426

42339CB00007B/457